*The Waving Gallery*

# Mervyn Taylor

# *The Waving Gallery*

Shearsman Books

First published in the United Kingdom in 2014 by
Shearsman Books
50 Westons Hill Drive
Emersons Green
BRISTOL
BS16 7DF

Shearsman Books Ltd Registered Office
30–31 St. James Place, Mangotsfield, Bristol BS16 9JB
(this address not for correspondence)

www.shearsman.com

ISBN 978-1-84861-330-0

ACKNOWLEDGEMENTS
Some of these poems have previously appeared in:
*Black Renaissance Noire, 2 Bridges Review, The St. Ann's Review, Taos Journal of Poetry and Art, Big City Lit.*, and ZocaloPoets.com.

I would like to thank Indran Amirthanayagam, for long-distance
discussions over time, about poems and poetry, Susana Case, for her
diligence, sharp eye and attuned ear, Ira Joel Haber, for teaching art
with a freeing mind, and Kathryn Weinstein, for letting me see
what the book would look like before it was finished.

# Contents

## Section 1. Leaving

## Section 2. Overstayed

## Section 3. In Transit

*For Lena*

# Section 1.

# Leaving

## Mt. Hololo

Let's talk, my friend,
when the wind comes
across the mountain
to touch our faces, and

flowers in your yard
rise on their stems
to salute, and the cock
puffs the feathers

round his neck, the
hens walking away
as if to say not again,
not today. Let's

talk about winters
in far-off lands, irate
husbands and windows
we jumped from,

let's brew the pack
and play a game of
rummy, though
neither of us is any

good. Show me
a painting you've
been working on
that may or may not

be going well. Let's
argue about a line,
a verse in a poem, the
cause of a fire that

has suddenly bloomed
on the hill. Let's leave
some issues for another
day, otherwise what

would we do tomorrow,
when your rooster's
tail grows too heavy for
his body, and the ladies

must remind him
when it's time to crow.
Let's discuss, until then,
important matters,

like the estimated
age of your eldest
turtle, like the day
that is dying outside.

# The Waving Gallery

Up there, I could make out my mother, in
her favorite dress, the one she wore in pictures
taken thirty years apart, and Doris, her friend

who'd warned her not to cry, a white kerchief
dabbing at her eyes. Behind them stood Uncle,
waving, the keys to the house and the Hillman

on the same ring. Across the tarmac the line
of travelers moved slowly, and the hills seemed
closer. I think I made out people in houses,

children in yards who could see me from that
distance, going away to study English, as if
it were not the language spoken here.

## First Time Seeing Snow

There's that scene in the movie when Sinatra
shuts off the wipers and floors the accelerator.

You're a passenger. You can't see a thing.
You hear the tick of ice, the whine of the motor,

and you think of the song he was singing
back in the bar, One for My Baby. You want

to say, *Don't do it, man. Doris loves you, the way*
*you turned when she answered the door, that hat.*

The car's an old Ford and in the theater your foot's
on the brake long after you've struck something,

and you sit there, Frankie slumped over the
steering, snow under the tires, churning.

## Country of Origin

Before going off to Argentina
on diplomatic duty,
the poet from Sri Lanka read to us
nervously. He told us how thieves

had broken into his car
and stolen his manuscripts.
Except for shoes, he had to
buy all new clothes, including
a silk shirt, which made him perspire.

That was before the twang of Spanish
spoken in Buenos Aires
took delight in its new trainee,
and his old habit of
pacing round the podium
entangled the streets like wires.

The mahout's in his office now,
patiently restoring his words.
Between appointments, and there
are many, he answers letters from
a new love, whose Tamil is just
as halting as his.

## Poet in Peru

It must be summer where you are,
your hands out of your pockets,
your scarf a neckerchief, more
for style than anything.
It must be steaming, sitting
outside that small café where
poets plead their cases for
Europe to be old again, and
America to fuck away with
those no-smoking laws. You're
pretending your coffee has
vodka in it, and that cursing is
the most natural thing. In that
village near the Equator,
your wife's temper assumes a
tragic air, one of screeches
and dives, like when parrots
pretend they can't find
home in the evening, and
grow so loud the poets point
in all directions, anything, just
to get them out of there.

# Edwidge's Voyage

I hear her singing, the policeman's boots
crunching near her hiding place. She is
quiet, then starts again, reading the
names of the missing, and the dead.

They don't recognize her in the cities,
grown woman whose smile is forever
young. She startles when she breathes,
the sharks that followed her scatter

in the wake of her song about hairless
women, and men who plunge
to their death convincing their children.
You may mark your place in her book

when you are done reading, you may
write your own. So says this woman
with the clearest of eyes. Buildings fall.
She ignores them.

## And Now This     *for Edwidge Danticat*


Sometimes it must feel like
your fight for independence
will never end, that liberty
will keep eluding you like
a goat that runs into the sea.

The preacher says it is your
voodoo that is killing you,
that keeps you scraping and
digging and having to subdue
the enemy in your own house.

But who can deny you your
home, where even in hunger
your mouths sing and drums
beat the sweetest ra-ra, eh?
Where your soldiers once

marched over the cliffs to
their death in the sea. And now
this, your roof falling in while
you were combing the children's
hair, sending them off to school,

while you were opening your stall
to sell the few grains that still
manage to grow, here comes
this rain of rocks upon your head,
this shaking of the ground, as if

God does not know his own
strength, as if He were dancing

carelessly in his house above
the mountains where your cries
would not reach.

Now from across the river
help comes. Who could
pretend not to hear such a
breaking up of earth, such
a split

run all the way from
Petionville to Jacmel, through
the belly of Port au Prince,
that where it ended it seemed
it could never be joined again.

A whole new island I tell you
is what you need, new roof,
new flooring, new everything,
new hills, new flowers new yard
with no fence to say

this is yours that is theirs,
someone forever claiming
what you work so hard for.
A place you can bring all those
Boat People back to, where

you can make a huge bonfire of
all the bad memories, of Papa
This and Baby That, the furry
slippers of their madams. But
never mind my wishes,

this is where you are now. This
is your sweet and sour, your
grief on top of grief, your little girl
dancing to show the amputation
was a success. Amazing how

you sing through your sorrow,
how you still fling your behind
in the Carnival when it comes,
and say your prayers however
you remember them, whatever

sacrifice you must make:
chicken, goat, your own blood,
saying, *Not me, not my Haiti,*
blood coming out of her pores.
Her mountains march naked

up and down beside the river
that divides the island as you
put it back together, the plate
that shifted the day the world
broke into a million pieces.

# Marie, and Juan

If he had remained in his country
and you in yours, you'd never
have danced like this.

He would never have crossed
the border between the cane,
nor known your name.

Your memory of Trujillo
would have focused your eyes
on the sharp edge of a machete

and your cries in patois
would have brought your father
running, the old Boukman record

skipping on the gramophone. But
here you are, dancing a bachata
in Brooklyn.

The step is fast,
the zombie from the past
trying to keep up.

# The Old Ways    *in memory of Achebe*

I would travel north to hear the great writer,
whose story about the champion wrestler
Okonkwo set the bar so high no rival
could take him down. And if my girlfriend

were still living there, I would spend the
weekend in Providence, recalling how hard
it is to find decent fish in a city so near
the sea. I could bear anything, the steep,

narrow staircase up to her bedroom, her
mattress on the attic floor. But now I hear
Chinua has died, I don't think I could stand
the memory of her roommates' chatter.

It brings to mind the children of the Evil
Forest, thrown there for being different. So
I stay home and reread how the hero chose
which wife, by placing his stool before her door.

# In the Act

*"After nearly half a century, denouncing brutality becomes a fairly circular enterprise."* — *From a review of Toni Morrison's* Home, *by Sarah Churchwell in* The Guardian, *April 2012.*

Maybe so, but I'm not ready to give up
on this lady, not ready to interfere with
mothers who won't let anyone near

their children, rather raise the rock
and smash them, if they must. Her
road to Paradise is the long way,

the uncorking of a bottle and realizing
it's not water, drunk before we know
the patter-roller's still dogging our step.

Write another, honey, how your boys
get through disguised as tumbleweed,
anything dead, that can't be killed twice.

The end of the novel is not your ending,
just breath you draw to begin again.
In a country full of dead-ends, you tell

of the need to turn around and find
some other way, a house in the distance,
a woman fetching firewood, building a fire.

## Single File        *for Brenda Connor-Bey*

Last night the stars came out
as never before, in clusters,
one in particular flaunting
its brilliance, its size. And we

interpreted this as a sign, as
powerless people tend to do, of
heaven's willingness to let us
have a few more minutes to say

what we have to say, to locate
an address that we once knew
by heart. And this is how we
come to *her* door, single file,

no one anxious to go in front
of the other, as in all her beauty
she slips out a window, shinnies
down the drainpipe, gone. Who,

for all our calling, won't come back,
will have us look up, on nights
like this, gazing at stars, believing
we know which one she is.

# What Poets Wish For

What poets wish for,
more than metaphors,
more than milk to feed
their cat, more than

a reprieve, is a trough
for horses that runs the
length of the town, a
gown for the serving

girl who brings a meal.
They live, these accused
perpetual liars of
whatever ages, behind

the bars of the brain,
within the turrets of
their hearts. And whoever
calls to them from the

outside must know, the
silence is not the sound
of the klaxon asleep at
his post, but an army of

clouds going by, sheep,
dragons wreathed in
smoke, a man on fire
leaping from the blaze.

# Section 2.

# Overstayed

## Student Days, DC

Leaving work at the Shoreham,
crossing the 16<sup>th</sup> St bridge that
leads from the hotel to our side
of town, we would harmonize

an old Sparrow song, "Darling
I can't remain," in February,
the city emptied by the myth
of Calypso, drawn to that

island at the end of the chain,
hung there like a charm, snow
falling as we tested the power
of the lyric to comfort, to keep

us warm, while what we really
wished for was to risk being
dashed against the rocks, to
get back for j'ouvert, darling.

# West Indian at the Front Desk

It took a long time for the new tenant's
furniture to arrive from Atlanta.
Every day she sat in the lobby looking out,
chain smoking and telling me all about
the move she was making. I listened,
and we ended up having an affair, which
began to sour the night I came to dinner
with books for classes the next day.
I'd assumed too much, she said.
It ended when someone in the building
threw a party, and my girlfriend
came by. I introduced them,
Virginia, meet Georgia, thinking
this is how it's done in America.

# Busboy

At the Shoreham in DC, where friends
got him a job, Blue never figured how
to slide the tray off his shoulder onto
the conveyor without breaking dishes.

There's a harshness to this country,
he said, after his girlfriend put him out
one very cold night, when one of her
Muslim sisterhood threatened to tell.

And in the School of Architecture,
those books, those hard courses,
calculus, and professors who frowned
upon students falling asleep in classes,

he tried, until once he went to work, not
realizing it was his day off. And that night
he dreamed of back home, and pumpkins.
Pumpkin, he said, coming out of his pores.

## Language Major

Underneath the Calvert Street Bridge, our
roommate Peter and a white woman who
looked younger in the bar, both tipsy, are
going at it. It's snowing hard, a postcard

scene, the stately Hotel Shoreham aglow,
and along the span at intervals, antique
streetlamps shining on black railings and
wet cobblestones. The sounds of Peter's

grunts echo in the underpass, the woman,
her coat and dress bunched at the waist,
suddenly declaring, she doesn't like Negroes.
"You're Spanish, aren't you?" she mutters.

And Dr. P (as we called him), ever mindful,
even in distress, whispers, "Sí, sí," snow
blowing off the steep embankment into
his ear, and onto his freezing behind.

# The Familiar

And after all this time I'm still
uneasy going into a place
full of white people, like that
bar in Coney Island, or the one
down in Maryland when I'd been
in the country only six months, and

the bartender said they didn't serve coloreds.
Or that time in Cape Cod forty years later
when I stumbled onto
what must have been a private beach,
the way the families looked up,
reaching for towels as if I'd

come upon them naked. Sometimes,
even now, in a friendly
place such as this, I still
find myself looking around,
noting the one black guy in the corner,
his reflection in the glass nodding, ok.

# Race                    *for Caitlin, again*


After we sped through that tunnel
of trees, after you led me in one of those sprints,
determined to prove your worth as a racer,

at last you slowed, and out of breath
I drew alongside, having managed to keep
your back fender in sight, because it's a strange town,

and I wouldn't have known where to turn,
which house without a confederate flag
to go to. And we stopped, and were taking pictures

when two of those hardcore riders yelled,
on the left, the left!, shooting us looks of
disdain in passing. I wanted to explain that,

although I was older, I was the amateur,
and had fallen twice that morning, forgetting
my feet were strapped in. How I survived

the twenty-seven miles without serious injury
was more your doing than mine. Cycling was once
simply how I got to school, and then

to work, not a contest. But your young, fit body
lifting your bike ahead of me up those narrow stairs
said everything American, competitive, prizes at the end.

# Concern

The forceps left two bruises
on my son's head, visible till
he was about six weeks old.

What kind of doctor, I ask,
grabs a kid like that, pulls him
like meat from the grill when

it's done? Two green spots,
as if the tongs were old, the
first thing they could find.

I find myself looking, now
the boy's forty, for further
signs of damage. So far, none.

# Benefit of the Doubt

There are galleries with pictures of
tigers among flowers, which perhaps
led the young man to jump into the
enclosure at the zoo, where the beast
lay drowsing in fall's lingering heat.

The spiked iron fence broke his pelvis,
and the tiger's tooth punctured the back
of his leg. The zookeeper said normally
they go for the neck, one good swing,
and there's meat for her cubs.

Last summer my grandson and I stared
at the creature through thick glass, those
eyes suggesting nothing like mercy.
"To be one with the tiger" may ring true,
like a temple bell in the mountains,

where even the air is holy. But caged,
in the city, boredom may have set in.
We'll go back to the museum and take
another look at that Rousseau, see if among
the blossoms there's any hint of a wink.

# The Last Round                    *for Neal*

This is what happened, after the doctors said
there was nothing more they could do, when
he had flown back and forth across the Atlantic.

He went home, and sold everything—furniture,
clothes, car. Opened the gate and let the
two Dobermans out—"Go, run for your lives!"

When he speaks now, his voice is a rasp, that
powerful body closed around it like a bell
around the clapper. His stance, too, is altered.

There's no fooling a fighter, especially the one
he faces now, who keeps his hood on till the last
minute, who closes in, knowing the dogs are gone.

# Mammogram

She didn't know, sitting there,
that the woman on her left
had one breast, that the one
on the right had none.

She just knew that
she had to take another test,
that something dark had
appeared in the picture.

Now they wanted a sonogram.
She sat and imagined the jelly
cold and efficient, the discs
stuck to her skin, the technician

making her turn on her side.
When they called her name
she arose slowly, went in,
undressed and put on

the open-front gown. Soon,
the suction cups made that sound.
The lab person was on the phone:
"Nothing. I don't see anything."

The women in the waiting room
looked up smiling. They seemed
perfect, all of them. Nothing
leaned, nothing fell down.

## Dry Eyes

Some people have dry eye,
some cry too much. Seems
they should share a tear or two,

sleep with eyelashes touching
and become aware
of one overflowing while

the other dreams of deserts,
a parade of animals
in search of water.

There are no doctors who
recommend this:
it occurred to me as you were

rubbing them raw
that your eyes could use
a good rain such as they

haven't seen in a long time,
like last year when
the water police came around

questioning the neighbors
about the flowers in my yard,
when the whole

savannah was parched and
much of the hills was
on fire.

## Another Country

After more than forty years
I saw them today, two sisters
who lived down the lane.

Wilma had had a stroke
and sat at the kitchen table,
clutching a padded heart.

They exclaimed how much
I resemble my mother now,
that they would not have

recognized me on the street.
I sat on the couch next to
Pearl, talking too much,

while on tv a soap opera
told the story of a man
leaving two lovers to go

off to war. We went through
the ranks of neighbors who
had lived on both sides,

the gay man whose hair dye
blackened the concrete
before his door, the dog that

followed children to church.
We spoke of illness, and
death, two subjects we'd

grown comfortable with,
of gout, and sugar,
the suicide of a girl we'd

thought too happy to die.
And Pearl pointed to a picture
of her mother in the foyer,

who'd adapted to snow
with hardly
any trouble at all.

# Shorty

The Spanish guy who lives downstairs
recently lost his wife. I used to see them
out front, her wheelchair angled against
the steps, his eyes tired from being up.

In my bad Spanish I'd offer, "Como estás?",
her "mucho dolor" turning the evening
purple, her hands on her knees. Since
her death he sits alone, announcing

he has a washing machine and dryer to sell.
And a freezer, he adds, arms extended
to show the dimensions, a gesture that
seems an offer to hug, the size of the pain.

## Settings

It's one thing to be lonely in
the city where glass looks down
on steel, where

there's artifice, a grand play
enacted every day, strangers
strolling on and off the avenues,
assured of their place, all eyes

focused on other things, the soul
an onlooker, uninvolved
in its own tragedy. But on
an island in a warm sea,

every leaf, every hill calls out
to its neighbor, begs for company,
will not leave you alone,
so loneliness becomes a creature

hard to hide under
an unrelenting sun, and even
harder at night, when other dogs
know your dog by name.

# Sedona

By now the desert air
should have calmed your fears.
Mine are still rock-hard,
if nothing else, good for building fences.
In Arizona, if I recall correctly,
standing close to the saguaro creates
a sense of euphoria. Have you done that yet?
When you lived at the Y on Lexington
in that cupboard of a room, you'd
cut the neck off a Pepsi bottle so I could pee.
I imagine where you are now I could stand
at your back door and spray the stars and send
the peccaries scooting back into the hills.

I picture your father, old army man
in his trailer with his collection of bottle caps,
what he would do if he ever saw my black behind
with your white legs wrapped around me,
what he would fasten the door with
so I couldn't leave, and your mother
closing up her gas station in Baltimore to spend
Thanksgiving with your brother in Virginia,
discussing your topless cleaning job, chastising
his wife for being startlingly overweight next
to her gelding son. I would come visit you
where you are now, far from the family,
closer to the meditative quiet you seek,

undoing whatever harmful side effects
years of medication have produced. But
never having gone to Pittsburgh where you sought
respite in the cold, and gurgled as you walked,

so much water did you drink, I doubt
I'll ever make it out to Sedona, out there,
among the spas and communes,
the retreats, the mountain mantras,
to take a deep breath and hold,
again, deep breath, and hold,
my road taking me in an opposite direction,
towards my folks and their silences,
where the water laps their shores.

# Storyteller

I go along with the story,
impossible as it is,
the book you wrote about us,
the surprise ending.

You are the one with
the imagination,
the mansion in Miami left you
by your mother, the one you fly to

every other weekend. You manage
a climax on every page, your characters
drunk and diving off piers that jetty
into oceans of turquoise.

I pretend to miss you going off
to Texas or Philadelphia, knowing full well
you are right there in your apartment smoking,
passing your tongue over your gold tooth

as you dream up a sequel
more fantastic than the last. For what is
lovemaking if not different every night,
if the stones do not mark us

so I look like a New Guinea tribesman,
you the tattoo woman whose lies disappear
once I leave the valley
where they are told.

# Speech

We left before the protests and
riots, only heard about raids
not far from where we grew up,
Big Jeff among those arrested.

While we were learning to battle
snowdrifts and subway crowds,
back home the boys were leading
marches that didn't have far to go,

every direction ending at the sea.
It's so when you live on an island:

the enemy is yourself, an Indian
with plenty mirrors dancing in the
Carnival, who whenever we return
throws down the challenge of

speech and spear, "O Warineh,
Warineh, di sam bokeh, Aieee!"
As we squirm in shame, having
forgotten the warrior's words.

# Section 3.

# In Transit

## Life in the Islands

They waited for the bird to appear
after the guide imitated its cry, but
there was only the rustle of leaves,
a fluffing of feathers and then,

silence. Still, it was worth the trip,
the tourists agreed, counting heads
to make sure they were all back
on the bus. There were murders

every day, they had been told,
and just yesterday, someone
had been shot on a busy street,
in the heart of the capital. In the

growing dark the salty sea-wind
let them know they were near
where the cruise ship had docked.
All around the city the hills twinkled

with lights, those tiny instances
that suggested windows, half-doors
looking into warm kitchens where
families they tried to picture, lived.

# Countryside

As many times as I've been there,
the roads remain strange, going east
when I think we're headed south,
passing fields of the same farmers
who lift and shake their heads.

I'm sure I was born here, though
when I hold out my hand the fish
swim away, the men toast someone
behind a partition, and only one
aunt claims she still loves me.

The spaces behind houses carry
the light in spare pockets, and
a quiet holds the hills like rakes
at lunchtime. I dare not ask which
trace leads to the sea, innocent

wave washing the same sand:
Manzanilla, Mayaro, Gasparee. Only
fifty square miles, but it can go on
forever, machetes looking for
something to cut, besides cane.

# Ecology

The poachers are sad,
drinking at that stand-up bar
along the Valencia stretch,
mourning the turtles
the backhoe destroyed.

What a broth they could have
made, a few eggs and fins
in brine and pepper. It would
have taken two at most
to make a man strong,

not the thousands gone
trying to turn the river away
from the hotel where tourists
are told to breathe quietly,
so as not to disturb the mother.

# Half an Island

I only know half of Haiti
from what she tells me,
the lady whose son
is stationed there.

The other half I know
from my friend the grimaux*
whose uncle went
to prison, and from

the men who argue
at the top of their voices
about everything
from football to torture,

who led the protest march
for Louima. There was one
dressed like death
who carried a red umbrella

and another who wore
rubber boots like a farmer
and waved
a rusty machete.

All day I followed them,
me and my friend the poet
who pointed out
that in their art

the paint is as thick
as blood and the women
in mourning are
still able to smile.

On an island split
down the middle
I discover the
stone that rattles

is really a heart.
And when the drums
go off in Prospect Park
and the horns blow,

next day I go
to find what they
buried in the circle
down by the lake,

those men who do
that fearsome dance
holding a black phone
with a cord that goes

nowhere, part fun,
part deadly serious,
who tremble like St. Vitus
with a roasting fever.

* light-skinned male

# The Mentor

I.
In this dream there were
cows in every field,
and clouds floating above
an island so green,

it seemed made of gases.
And out of this arose the
poet, in a grey suit,
as spry as I've ever

seen him, quoting his
mischievous lines,
tieless, sparkling with
metaphor, asking his trick

question—are you coming
with me, are we going
to find reasons? Not
in this place, I answered,

where no one should ever
starve, or complain about
things other than a gate
left open through which

a calf might wander
and be stolen,
causing dispute
settled in devious ways.

## II.

You remember Lena.
In the dream she too
was present, wearing
a hat like a teakettle cover,

remarking those boys who
live where she grew up,
tattooing their bodies,
a young girl every Friday

hosting a perfume sale.
It is rumored this is the
house an outpatient
was looking for, when

he went to the wrong
address and used
a wheelbarrow handle to
beat a bedridden 90 yr. old

to death, next door those
who harbored the one
he was seeking saying
not a word, their weapons

like marshmallows in their
pockets, hands over their
ears, blocking the sound of
bones breaking, and screams.

## III.

Cows crop the grass,
brown and white backs
seen from above, the land
in undulating waves below.

Out of the few houses,
people in black following
funerals, fathers refusing
to accept each other's

apologies. They turn their
backs, have conversations
with their dead sons as they
are lowered, earth tamped.

Ah, the poet smiles his
ineffable smile; those adverbs
he warned against shuffle up.
What will we do with them,

now that he is going, trailing
long verses, the islands strung
like cans behind a wedding,
bells pealing in chapels

whose stone walls he tries
to rebuild, Sunday's
blood in silver chalices,
the host held high,

the priest's voice intoning
the liturgy—sunlight, stained
glass, sin, in sonorous
four-by-four refrain.

IV.
This is where they reenact
the story of sacrifice,
with animals, gold
and greed, where

the washing of hands
goes on, governors
and guards swearing
each other away, poets

swearing out poems like
warrants, charges read
in the language of verse,
the one in gray citing

history and places
in the landscape that
hold titles and deeds,
the right to dream.

# Returning

We're back from the sea
salt in our hair
sand in our shoes

This time we did not
cross the ocean
but came out the way
we went in

Still native
Still island
Still retracing

our own steps
to see where we
made that turn

that made us spend
all those years saying
goodbye.

# Somewhere Safe

Here, where the wheels of the car
spun in the sand, this is where
we should have stayed, the beach bums
helping us chuckling under their breath,
that paradise of love and sandflies,
where we went as soon as I got
my driver's license.

Here are the pictures, posed
in front of flowerbeds in The Gardens,
parked by the gates of rich houses in St. Clair,
annoyed by the peeper whose head
came out behind us, smiling,
like a family member,
sharing the experience.

And here's that spot in the savannah where
we heard the policeman's mumbled warning
when he wasn't sure what to arrest us for.
His horse's belly big and gray,
his torchlight shining in our eyes,
we waited for the apparition to move,
so we could continue.

We set out, night after night, days too,
looking for a safe place, somewhere
hidden but from where we could
still see lights, and people,
where the conch shells piled on the beach
could become part of memory's landscape,
some of its indelible sprawl.

# The Devil's Chariot

Headley McClachlen, Gospel Hall Pastor, when
my great aunt asked what kind of car she should get,
said the automobile was the devil's chariot. But he
and his sons had three of those deuce and a quarter
winged ones lined up in the church driveway, the
ladies checking their hats and faces in the mirrors
as they squeezed by, their husbands remarking
that the steering columns were on the left. And

later, church over, the dashboard lit up, the stations
Spanish from nearby Venezuela, French from Saint
Lucia, he wondered what made Charlotte think she
could afford one, what she thought of his warning
about the devil. But the bright sashay of her dress,
her bangles resting on her grandchildren's shoulders
said nothing, not even good evening as he drove by,
radio blaring, the caravan of his sons following.

# The Body Politic

There's a spill in the country now,
like milk from the breasts of women
who drank too much vervine,

like oil in the Gulf of Paria,
a mother running her hands over
the body of a slain son. There's

nothing to catch the grief: one
doctor in attendance, one
security guard, whole families

going through corridors carrying
a feverish child. Outside, cars race
and turn screeching where posts

have been put up to keep them
from flying into the sea.
There's nothing to stop the fury

with which men go after each other,
pour kerosene and light matches,
overhead wires crackling. And still,

one holds his newborn, among the
chives and pumpkins on market day,
the body politic skinned in the square.

## Carnival Takeover

Men used to teach women how
to sing of abuse and smile, how
to back them up in calypso and
make audiences roll with laughter,

how to hold the wooden penis
and pretend it belonged to them.
Now those men have become the
drunks they portrayed, and

the sailors once invited to steal
panties off the lines are gone,
ships chugging out the harbor,
the ladies having declared war.

# In Crazy Port of Spain     *for Adelina, again*


An electric wire fell on her
and burned her

In crazy Port of Spain General
when she spoke Spanish someone
called her foreign
said send her away

And in Stafford Court where
she took care of her mother

they tried to dispossess Adelina
who would have died had not
a passer-by seized the black snake
of a cable still sparking
moved it away from her body till it lay

on the ground angry at her
for rushing home
to make lunch forgetting to
look up in this city that was once friendly
now strung with boots and things
that could fall and things that go off
behind a lamppost or dustbin

In crazy Port of Spain how much more
careful could she be walking up
Henry Street on a beautiful Tuesday morning

wondering what to cook
for the old lady today

## Layover Trinidad

In transit to New York
Zamir the Guyanese
not knowing it was Carnival
searched Port of Spain for

a place to stay and ended up
spending the night on a chair
in a hotel lobby
after the night clerk

came to his rescue when
he found himself surrounded by
painted men with pitchforks
demanding money.

## Post Mistress

Don't mail anything here.
They haven't revised
the old way of sorting.
Your last package arrived
months late, opened with
a scribbled note,
Damaged in Handling.
I've come to rely on
local delivery: a neighbor
crossing the street with bread
baked an hour ago.

# John Creig, Esq. of Woodford Square

1.
He came in his rags
to the post office, letter
addressed to the Queen.

He had just enough for postage,
everyone declaring his
handwriting, how wonderful.

How long, he asked,
would it take to get there?

Four weeks, said the clerk,
placing the letter
where all crazy correspondence

went, in a bin
filled to the top.


2.
He is the gentleman in rags
who keeps writing the Queen
that she should come and see
the legacy slavery has left.

*My dear Britannia*, he writes,
in hope that one day she might
answer, perhaps follow with
a visit to his cardboard home,

if only to see the source of such
great penmanship, to hear the
complaints of those who put up
to buy him a suit last Easter.

# Diplomat from Peru

You have just enough time
to watch the kiddies parade,
and then you must go back
to that place of high elevation

where for water they depend on
the runoff from the Andes.
We don't notice how drunk you are
till you grow dizzy watching

the girl play tenor in the steelband.
You will tell them about this,
the somber stories of our country
not belying, how this instrument

made you forget your duties,
domestic and public,
sending you onto the plane
clapping, and waving our flag.

## Steelband Clash

Those men in the shadow of the
memorial in Protest Square in Cairo
remind me of that Carnival when
Desperadoes clashed with Sunland,
and we hid under the stairs of an optometrist,
turning our t-shirts inside out.

In the same way these two discard
their chains of office, drop them
into the dried-up fountain, looking
for the safest route out of the city, though
given the crowds and the smoke,
there couldn't be one.

They were probably all like the street
where, making our escape, we saw Fred,
limping, his knee the size of a melon,
and heard about the height of the wall
he had had to scale.

## Stella

In old age she has become
as fluent in Spanish as she was
when she was twenty, still living in
that village south of Caracas. Her

children, all grown up, are amazed
at how she keeps their uniforms
starched and ironed, as if someday,
they might go back to school.

And her husband Charles, who first
taught her English, observes, with his
sharp policeman's eye, how she has
shrunk to just below his pocket, she

who used to see eye to eye with him
on everything, including never using
profanity in front of the children, now
saying, "Besa mi culo," to all of them.

## Widow's Peak

It comes to the edge
of the forehead,

that diving wedge, the
sign of a man who

will outlive his wife.
My father had one,

a plunging arrowhead
aligned with his nose.

Stubborn to the end,
he went first,

a cynic who had
no faith in signs.

## Facing Montrose

We moved when I was five,
to a house diagonally
across the street with
an iron bathtub in the yard.

We carried things by hand,
the light stuff my mother and I,
the big press my uncle and
a man in a heavy jacket.

It was temporary, until
my father finished building the one
in the lane, facing Montrose.
Careful with the teapot, my mother

said, excitement ringing her eyes.
Would we bathe outside, for all
the neighbors to see, would
my father finally, after parking

his bike in the new yard,
hang his uniform behind the
door and stay, instead of riding
away, down the hill in the dark?

# The Party

My cousin celebrated his birthday
on a Monday, when
we retirees could sit and
listen to a legacy of calypsos,
naming them, and the singers.

And we ate, and told stories,
toasting our aches and pains,
he with failing sight
taking up the wrong glass
and going to check on

his mother, who lay in a back room
stripped in the noonday heat
calling his name, the dog under
the veranda, whose chain
rattled, reaching for the bones.

# Ticks

The workmen have packed up and gone,
under the house the ticks buried beneath
three inches of concrete. So small

and yet, they take everything we've got,
and keep coming back. The slugs choose
midnight as their invading hour, the gardener

with a lamp and a handful of salt slipping
in their slime and off to the hospital, his skull
split open. I guess they'll have their way,

the little things that annoy us, and
remain, long after we give up, the yard,
the garden gone to ruin. In the meantime

the workmen will return on Monday,
the old man quarreling with the young,
who doesn't see what the problem is.

# Both Blind

My cousin slings
his mother over his shoulder.
It's the only way to get her
to take a bath. Once she's

dressed, to keep her from
stripping, he tapes
her clothes on. It doesn't help.
Soon, she's naked again.

She calculates in nine years
she'll be a hundred.
Nine more years?
By then he'll be eighty!

Drying her off
he remarks her breasts
feel flat, almost woven,
like alpargatas.

Well, that's something,
she coos, from deep in the
towels he swaddles her in,
that's still something.

## No Owner

Without an owner the goat
travels far, rubs up against
a tree, by its roughness
knows what country he's in.

This is not home. He would
have seen the sea by now.
Must be Russia, by the curl of
the male's horns, the rutting

cry of the female. There's
poetry among the vodka
crowd. They don't insist
on currying everything.

They call him Vanya, or
some such name, who must be
a good person. No one
ties a rope around his neck.

## What Will Happen

What will happen to the cow
when the new highway
comes through, what

about the house old man
Roblee built, the shade trees
he planted, the bulldozer that

sits almost on his grandchildren's
back step, the strange men
eating sandwiches in the noon-

day sun. What will happen
to the field, now visible from
every window, what

about the one protester
starving himself, his ribcage
on the front page. What

about the cow, her mooing making
what the prime minister is telling
the man's mother impossible to hear.

## Mother Moon

A child cries outside the door
of the locked house, the clock
ticking away the curfew hour.
Finally, the mother lets him in.

But tomorrow, she will hand in
the keys of kindness, put the grater
in the middle of the yard and
make him kneel, while the moon,

hiding from her mischief, floats
in the bath of a cloud, laughing
at the brick the child holds aloft,
the sister's dress he's wearing.

# Folding Chairs

Because he did not approve,
the stepdad
sat in his van outside the hall

and waited till they were done
with the rented tables and chairs,
refusing to come in for anything,

just sat there, their joy not the joy
he'd pictured, not the one she
was dancing with,

having just made their vows.
In his van he sat for hours,
doing his duty, waiting until

it was time to take back
the tent, after they were
done with it, the dishes, his life.

# Embassy

I walk around the savannah,
sometimes early enough to see
the applicants for visas
lined up in the dark.

Most of them won't get through.
They'll forfeit the application fee
and go home dejected, postponing
the long-distance call to Brooklyn.

I sit among them in a bar and watch
the news from Libya and Cairo,
how they burn flags and lob
grenades, while here the locals

finish their petit quarts and ask
when will they fix the bridge
up the road, and how long did
it take me to get mine.

# Home from America

Driving through villages he witnessed
a Sunday full of worship: Muslims
in white, Christians in hats and flowers,
early drinkers whom he acknowledged

as they turned on their stools and bowed.
This is what he came back to the island for,
the warmth, the wash of light upon the faces
of the faithful, the pace slower than

a hammock's swing. Eventually he reached
his uncle's house, and home from service the
family looked up, giving him the chair under
a painting of a farm during a hard winter,

animals in the snow, as if to make him feel
at home, and the heavy quilt on the bed
in the front room where the sun came in,
where he napped the entire afternoon.

# Breath

Sometimes I can still
smell my father's breath

coming out of his body,
especially when

I sneeze,
his earned power

entering my nostrils
in full,

round puffs, with
a base of tarnished copper.

If my son were to
huddle with me now,

under the weight of his
own fatherhood, he might

catch a hint of magnesium
stirred under the collarbone,

a mix of tea, and filings
from the rails on which

his grandfather's train
traveled and sparked

through cane fields,
filling him, to the brim.

## How I Can Tell   *for Samantha*


You must be from that place
full of caves that echo Gasparee, and
where, when it rains, Aranguez floods.

In your voice I hear rivers
fill up, the sea
coming back for more.

You must have gone running
down Aripo's steep sides, its tongue-tied
villagers calling after you, don't go,

don't go, just before
they started drinking
rubbing alcohol.

Ah, girl from between mountains,
you came away, your passage
booked by someone

who must have heard
the choir in old
St. Margaret's church singing,

someone who wanted to
pass you through
the world's cities first, before

you spread wild like tannia,
the leaf that overgrows
the roads back home.

## Enchanted Evening

When I used to sing that song, it
would start such a racket among
the neighborhood pets, a screech
from the parrot with a stroke, howls
from the dog, the near-human cries
of cats. But you, my dear, sink into
your favorite chair, close your eyes,
become whomever I need you to be,
the lady who encouraged me to dance,
the young girl in a hat and nothing else
who leads the way around the table,
saying don't stop, as at some point
we drift into the furniture, and I hum
the refrain into your hair, into your
skin, while the rest of the world
strains to hear how it will end.

www.ingramcontent.com/pod-product-compliance
Lightning Source LLC
Chambersburg PA
CBHW030048100426
42734CB00036B/579